STRONG
FAITH

Daily Encouragement for Moms
& Families of Premature Babies

STRONG
FAITH

*Daily Encouragement for Moms
& Families of Premature Babies*

Jamie C. Johnson

DEDICATION

To Our source: God

My love: Joshua

My lovey: Caleb

My nephew: Dawson

Uncle Donnie

Aunt Cathy

My love for you all is endless.

To my sisters, the mothers of premature hospitalized babies:
You are not alone!

Contents

Foreword

With the ring of the phone, panic ensued in our immediate family when we received the news that Jamie was in labor with Caleb eight weeks early. After a devastating loss just days prior, at that moment, our strength was sapped. We didn't feel equipped to handle another trial, and it was difficult to stay positive.

However, I am my sister's keeper, and I knew Jamie needed love and support. We are one year apart in age and have a twin-like connection. This may sound odd, but while miles apart, I knew she was striving to muster up all the faith she had in order to persevere and believe her son would live and thrive. I could spiritually discern her internal fight. She was aiming to uphold continuous optimism while defeating doubt and worry that attempted to rise up as she vocalized God's promises without ceasing.

Like you, Jamie was faced with complex decisions from the moment Caleb was born. Each time the doctors entered the room, she had to distinguish between what she would receive as *news* and updates versus what she would receive as *truth*. I was there to support her as she determined what advice to accept or reject, which words to rebuke or agree with, and which hospital visits or lack thereof to be at peace with. With joy and no longer accepting despair, I now recognize that my sister and brother-in-love were in an *uphill* battle. I am so thankful the battle was not theirs to fight, and in the end, there was victory! God brought Caleb into the world right on time, though *we* considered his birth premature.

As you are the parent(s) of an early gift (premature Little One), this devotional is for you! If you are serving as a support, this devotional is for you too! You are on this journey also, and you need to be encouraged and fortified. Jamie and our family members have walked in your shoes. You can trust she understands every sentiment you are experiencing. With love and care laced through the words of this devotional, Jamie will speak to your heart and share words of affirmation, inspiration, and support that will help you stand strong in this season.

Your Little One is more resilient than you can imagine.

My prayer is that as you read this devotional, you see your Little One as healthy and whole. I also pray that you experience the love of Christ and receive His joy that surpasses all understanding.

I thank God for choosing Jamie and Joshua to birth Caleb and for positioning her to empower you for such a perfect time as this!

Monica C. Darden, MA

Opening Letter to You, My Sister

Dear Sis,

You have experienced the wonderful gift of giving birth to one of God's Little Ones! I'm sure your Little One's arrival has likely set a lot of things in motion that you weren't necessarily prepared for. Like a game of tennis, you are experiencing the joy that comes with seeing your baby face-to-face and fear of the unknown. Many other women, including me, have been in your shoes, so I think it's safe to say that what you're experiencing is normal.

As you are reading this devotional, I encourage you to welcome God's comfort and peace into your heart. Allow Him to meet you where you are, knowing that He loves you. He has your back because He cares for you and your Little One.

I penned the words in this book specifically for you: to inspire you, lift you up, give you hope, strengthen you, and keep your mind in perfect peace while sharing Scriptures that you can trust. (See Isaiah 26:3–4.)

This devotional is designed for a thirty-one-day consecutive flow; however, you are welcome to dive into the entries in the order that fits your needs. You will notice a pattern in the layout. Each topic is divided into two parts. First, you will be immersed in words of encouragement. You'll read a brief yet relevant story and encounter Scriptures of God's promises plus a powerful declaration you can proclaim boldly to build your faith. On the following day, you'll have space to reflect. These are action days. I've provided space for you to journal your thoughts, feelings, experiences, and prayers.

Every week, you will find a section to document your wins, answers to prayers, and your victories (WAVs-pronounced waves). But you don't need to wait until you get to that day to write your WAVs. Record them whenever you'd like.

As you're reading, remember I'm on this journey with you. You are not alone. Moreover, God is with you. The road ahead won't always be easy, but I pray that your faith is built up as you embrace each Scripture and embark upon the reflection activities. Know that I carefully crafted each writing prompt and shared every word of encouragement with honor and love.

I am excited about the possibilities and outcomes throughout our devotional journey together. Before we start, I must mention that this book is not a substitute for professional help. If you need someone to talk to about your experience with your Little One, I encourage you to seek the appropriate help for you. You can start by talking with someone you trust, your doctor, your pastor, or a counselor. You are not alone!

I thank you for being willing to be open and become vulnerable throughout this faith-building process. Though we do not know each other personally, I call you my sister because we have a shared experience: caring for a premature Little One.

Written with love.

Your sister,
Jamie

Introduction

It was a normal day after work. Joshua and I were grabbing a few items at Walmart to hold us over between weekly grocery shopping trips. As we were heading to the checkout, I suddenly felt a pressure, equivalent to the feeling of urination, release. I stopped right in my tracks. As Joshua was now a few more steps ahead of me, I said, "Love, Love," as he glanced back at me, wondering what was wrong. "I think my water broke." In my mind, I kept asking myself if it *really* happened. *How could I be sure?* It was too early in my pregnancy, and we hadn't discussed this scenario during my midwife appointments. I wanted to believe what I was feeling was the result of a weak bladder. *It's common, right?* But I knew I hadn't felt the urge to go to the bathroom.

Joshua was a little freaked out although, previously, he played it cool and said he'd be ready for Caleb whenever the time came. I went to the bathroom to see what was going on, and the water wouldn't stop flowing. I wiped myself, but I couldn't get the water to stop. I left the bathroom and told my Love that, in fact, my water had broken. His eyes nearly bulged out of his head! He left the cart in the middle of the aisle and grabbed my hand, and we headed for the door. As we entered the car, I realized that we weren't ready; *I* wasn't ready. I told him to take us home so that I could get the information I needed for the midwife department at the hospital. However, because of rush hour, we encountered horrible traffic. I quickly changed my mind and decided we should head to the hospital because I wasn't sure how much time we had. I Googled the midwives' department and learned it was closed. I called the after-hours number and paged the midwife on call. I began to panic and pray silently. I was trying to stay calm while sitting in the passenger seat as the water continued to flow. I kept feeling waves of pressure, then an intense release. It was uncontrollable!

When we arrived at the hospital, Joshua found a wheelchair and took me to the information desk because we had no idea where we were going. We hadn't gone over that either during my midwife appointments because the projected delivery date was months away. After much back and forth, the clerk told us where to go. We arrived at the triage only to be flooded with numerous questions as the ocean of water continued to flow from my body, temporarily pool in my seat, and eventually trickle down my legs.

I was finally taken to a room and asked to change my clothes. I changed as best as I could. I needed Joshua to help me. My dress and shoes were soaked and needed to be bagged. Part of me was embarrassed because the water wouldn't stop. I kept talking to God in my head while trying to stay calm because I had no idea what was going on. I often said I was ready for Caleb to make his entrance, but I knew thirty-two weeks was way too soon for his arrival. I slid into the bed and had a short wait until a nurse came in. While waiting, I initiated small talk with Joshua about how to get in touch with my co-worker to let him know that I wouldn't be in the next day. I was supposed to be hosting and leading a celebration workshop for a group of teaching artists, and I had all the supplies in my car! I had to take my mind off what was going on, so I focused on work instead.

Eventually, a slew of nurses and doctors came in. I was slightly annoyed because they asked me the same questions that I had been asked by triage and the answers were already in my chart. Moreover, I just had an appointment at the hospital three days prior. The professional staff told me that I needed an ultrasound, and at best I would need to stay in the hospital a few days so that I could make it to thirty-four weeks. The other option was an emergency cesarean section. At that time, I had barely dilated to one centimeter. I thought for sure that I'd be able to wait and deliver Caleb at a later date. That all changed after the ultrasound. Caleb wouldn't move so that his muscle tone could be assessed. I had lost too much fluid for him to wait another day. His heart rate dropped a few times, and to top it off, he was breech. When the technician told me that Caleb had turned, I couldn't believe it. I wondered if his movement was what I felt when I thought I was experiencing a contraction. Immediately after receiving this report, I was wheeled off for an emergency cesarean section.

Within twenty minutes, we were parents! I couldn't believe it. I was a mom. Shocked yet grateful, I stayed in a mode of prayer and confession the entire time. I had to believe that our son was healthy even though he was born two months early. I was nervous. I needed visual confirmation that Caleb was okay. The doctors only allowed me to see him for a brief moment before rushing him to the neonatal intensive care unit. I had to wait for the epidural to wear off before I could go to the NICU to see him. Joshua was allowed to see him while I was recovering, so he took pictures of Caleb for me.

While I was in my room alone, I declared aloud that Caleb was "God's first." I had to believe that Caleb belonged to Him and He was God's beautiful creation given to us at the perfect time.

DAY 1

A Gift from God

*I prayed for this Little One, and the Lord
granted me what I asked of him*
(1 SAMUEL 1:27).

Congratulations, Sis! Whether this is your first time giving birth or not, I believe in celebrating each time a Little One is born.

I was filled with anticipation while I waited to see Caleb. Though I planned for a natural birth, inevitably, I needed an emergency cesarean section. Nervousness aside, I thought my experience would be similar to what I had seen in movies and on television; after giving birth the doctor would allow me to hold my newborn baby. Not in my case. Caleb was immediately placed in an incubator. Anxiety increased as I waited for what seemed to be forever to hear him cry. Once I heard him, I was flooded with relief. A nurse wheeled Caleb over to Joshua and me. Tears flowed down my face, and I grabbed Joshua's hand tightly. I was trying to be strong, but I had a difficult time because all I wanted to do was hold him. A mother is supposed to hold her baby once they enter the world. Why couldn't I? I was saddened by the reality of how unfair it was to only have seconds with my son and then

1

watching him being wheeled away to a room with people he didn't know.

When I made it to my room after surgery, my mother and oldest sister met me. They excitedly congratulated me; however, I was almost numb. I found it hard to celebrate right then. I fought against feelings of guilt, shame. and blame for Caleb's early arrival.

Finally, I could see Caleb. Seeing him changed everything. In an instant, I felt honored. *I* was chosen as the mother to bring this precious Little One into this world. I thanked God repeatedly for being able to see the precious face of the life that had been growing inside me. I know it's challenging for you as the arrival time of your Little One didn't happen when planned, but I encourage you to celebrate being the mother of a gift from God.

HIS PROMISES

"Every good and perfect gift is from above"
(JAMES 1:17).

Gifts come in different sizes and in diverse beautiful wrappings. Regardless of your Little One's weight, health, and circumstances, you've been given a gift directly from God. As women of faith, we know that we cannot rely solely on what we see with our natural eyes. Your Little One may be small, but see their perfection. Health concerns may exist, but see them as a wonderful blessing.

"Children are a gift from God, they are His reward"
(PSALM 127:3).

At times in life, we receive "surprise" gifts. For me, not only was Caleb's early arrival shocking, but my pregnancy was a surprise too. Caleb wasn't planned. Early on, I had moments of denial. As time progressed, my denial transformed into love. Being the receiver of such a precious gift from God is an honor and a privilege I encourage you not to take lightly. Your Little One is the manifested proof that God heard your prayer and desire. Recognizing that God heard you develops your faith. It's not a matter of receiving your reward in your timing but in God's perfect timing.

TODAY'S DECLARATION

As I pray for (Little One's Name) I believe the Lord will grant me what I ask of Him. (Little One's Name) is a good and perfect gift from above. (Little One's Name) is a gift from God, he/she is His reward.

DAY 2

Sister Talk & Reflection

It is an honor and privilege to give birth to God's gift. Describe what you love most about your Little One.

_____

_____

_____

_____

_____

_____

_____

_____

_____

_____

_____

_____

_____

_____

_____

_____

_____

WHAT'S ON MY HEART & MIND

_____

_____

_____

_____

_____

_____

_____

_____

_____

_____

_____

_____

_____

_____

_____

_____

_____

_____

_____

_____

_____

PRAYERS

_____

_____

_____

_____

_____

_____

_____

_____

_____

_____

_____

_____

_____

_____

_____

_____

_____

_____

_____

_____

_____

_____

DAY 3

His First

*Before I formed you in the womb, I knew you,
before you were born I set you apart
(JEREMIAH 1:5).*

Seeing your Little One in an incubator can weigh on you. You feel as if there's nothing you can do to help them. Tubes and wires are everywhere. Machines with lines and numbers that you don't understand. Sounds and beeps are coming from the machines that are far from comforting. You're probably thinking, *How can I be a mother to my Little One if all I can do is touch them through openings in a plastic container, and when I can hold them, I must be careful of the wires?* I'm sure you find yourself becoming so obsessed and concerned with the fluctuation of the numbers and sounds that you forget to focus on the quality of your time together. In addition, your time is shared with doctors, nurses, specialists, family, and friends. You know they all play a vital role, but when do you get to have your Little One to yourself? You find yourself worrying about everything. You have so much to learn, know, and repeat every time you're asked a question. You might even feel responsible for your Little One's situation, and you want to assist in their growth and development so that they can come home.

The truth is, your Little One belongs to God first, and He has everything taken care of. He was with your Little One before they were born, while they were developing in your womb, and He is still present! In the previous entry, we talked about how your Little One is a gift from God. Gifts must originate from somewhere. In this case of giving birth, your baby originated from God. I had to realize my own desires were selfishly motivated and when I thought about my wants, it was no longer about Caleb. If I wanted to remain focused on what he *needed*, I had to walk in the truth of knowing that Caleb belonged to God first and he was gifted to me as his mother. I was a blessed vessel chosen to birth him, and my job was to *believe,* nurture, and love while God took care of His Little One (Caleb).

HIS PROMISES

> *"For you created my inmost being; you knit me*
> *together in my mother's womb. I praise you because*
> *I am fearfully and wonderfully made"*
> (PSALM 139:13).

God wants you to know that He has been present since the beginning. How amazing is it to know that God cares so much that He made sure it was written to you in His Word! There is a relationship between your Little One and God—the ultimate relationship between Father and child. Think about the care you have for your Little One. Now multiply your love by infinity. That's how much God cares.

"The Lord himself goes before you and will be with you; he will never leave you nor forsake you. Do not be afraid; do not be discouraged" (DEUTERONOMY 31:8).

Despite all the many forms of distractions that instill fear and doubt in your mind, remember that because your Little One is God's first, He will always be there for them. Hold on to this promise, especially when you can't be with your Little One. The promise that God will never leave nor forsake your Little One supersedes the qualifications of the medical professionals involved in your Little One's care.

TODAY'S DECLARATION

Before You formed my Little One in my womb, You knew them, and before they were born, You set them apart.

DAY 4

Sister Talk & Reflection

It's amazing to know that your gift came directly from God.
Describe how you feel knowing that your Little One is His
first.

_____

_____

_____

_____

_____

_____

_____

_____

_____

_____

_____

_____

_____

_____

_____

WHAT'S ON MY HEART & MIND

PRAYERS

_____

_____

_____

_____

_____

_____

_____

_____

_____

_____

_____

_____

_____

_____

_____

_____

_____

_____

_____

_____

_____

DAY 5

Trusting God

*Trust in the Lord with all your heart; do not
depend on your own understanding*
(Proverbs 3:5).

Trusting God daily is a must. Your Little One may be experiencing challenges; however, progression and healing is possible! I visited Caleb every day, and upon my arrival, I would get an update from a nurse. They would tell me how Caleb was doing, how he was overnight, and what the NICU team had decided about his course of treatment. Our meetup was also my time to ask questions. I asked what their notes meant in his daily log book and made sure I understood their medical jargon. Since Caleb was born two months early, he had to learn a lot of things quickly. An important function was the ability to breathe and swallow at the same time. Whenever he experienced difficulty doing so, his heart rate and oxygen levels dropped, and the alarm on his monitor sounded off. One of the first things the nurses reported to me was the number of alarms. Hearing the number of times my baby's levels dropped scared me. I was frightened each time it happened while I was holding him. I had to quickly remember that Caleb was God's son who was gifted to me, which meant I had to trust God with Caleb's

17

care. I had to trust that the individuals caring for Caleb in the NICU had been divinely placed there by God. If I noticed a specific person that did not have his best interests in mind, I declared that they would no longer be a part of his daily care team. Trusting God is a concept that may seem oxymoronic. Displaying this trust requires you to remain still while "doing." The stillness is the confidence you have in God, and the doing is speaking God's truth.

Because your trust is in God, I encourage you not to solely rely on your own understanding or depend on the finite understanding of those around you, medical staff included. I am certainly not suggesting that you totally disregard professional opinions. What I mean is, if they give you a report about your child that you are not in agreement with (i.e. it doesn't align with your spirit), you don't have to receive it as the ultimate truth. Place your trust in God. Know that He will take care of it because it's a concern of yours.

HIS PROMISES

"You will keep in perfect peace all who trust in you, all whose thoughts are fixed on you! Trust in the Lord always, for the Lord God is the eternal Rock" (ISAIAH 26:3–4).

Maintaining your peace is essential. Peace already belongs to you, and it will remain when you fully trust God by focusing on Him rather than the circumstances. Allow God to be the rock and refuge that He is. When you let His love surround you, His peace will fill you.

"Be strong and courageous do not be afraid; do not be discouraged, for the Lord your God will be with you wherever you go"
(JOSHUA 1:9).

Trusting God definitely takes strength and courage because you are giving your all to someone you cannot see with your natural eyes. The beautiful thing is that God makes His presence known by proving Himself time and time again! That's why He doesn't want you to fear or be troubled by the circumstances before you.

TODAY'S DECLARATION

I trust in You, Lord, with all my heart; and I will not depend on my own understanding.

DAY 6

Wins, Answers to prayers, & Victories

Trusting God is an act of surrender. Use the space below to share what you're trusting God for.

_____

_____

_____

_____

_____

_____

_____

_____

_____

_____

_____

_____

_____

_____

_____

_____

WHAT'S ON MY HEART & MIND

WINS, ANSWERS TO PRAYERS, & VICTORIES

_____

_____

_____

_____

_____

_____

_____

_____

_____

_____

_____

_____

_____

_____

_____

_____

_____

_____

_____

_____

_____

DAY 7

Setting the Atmosphere

Worship the Lord with gladness;
come before him with joyful songs
(Psalm 100:2).

The room where your Little One is staying is a holy place of worship. If you don't perceive it as such right now, know that you have the power to transform the atmosphere. When Caleb was in the NICU, I walked around Caleb's hospital room praying. It was my way of connecting with God. In addition, it was the perfect time to verbalize my declarations regarding his health and my beliefs. Confessing God's Word and worshipping Him gave me strength in my moments of weakness. I believe you will be strengthened as you do the same. What I am suggesting you do can be considered easier said than done; however, I am sharing this with you because I was in your shoes and it *can* be done. I have initiated many unorthodox things, such as talking to the machines in the room while praying. I told the machines what they would and would not do to and for my son. Most days, my prayer time evolved into a powerful worship experience in the NICU.

I am a worshiper at heart, and I love worship music. No slight to any other genre, but worship music is enveloping. Worship music often makes me feel as if I am at the feet of God. Creating this type of atmosphere can help your trust increase. If you're a worshiper, I'm sure you have a favorite worship song or two. If you can, play it softly so that your Little One can hear it. If you can't, consider playing it through your earbuds. Sing along with the track so the lyrics can saturate the space of the room. You don't have to be a great singer. The focus is on creating an atmosphere of peace and miracles in your Little One's room while ministering to their soul. Remember, you are worshiping from a stance of victory. Prayer and pure worship is your weapon when anxiety or any other trick of the enemy tries to creep into your heart.

HIS PROMISES

> *"Sing to the Lord, for he has done glorious*
> *things; let this be known to all the world"*
> (ISAIAH 12:5).

While worshiping, you can thank God for all He's done for you and declare His goodness. If you're not a singer, your times of worship may encompass speaking the promises of God. When they are spoken in faith and with confidence, it is as if you are singing a song. It's like a sweet-smelling savor unto God.

*"The Lord is my strength and my shield; my heart
trusts in him, and he helps me. My heart leaps
for joy, and with my song I praise him"*
(Psalm 28:7).

The joy you experience during your time of worship is
evidence of your confidence in Him. Your worship releases
your faith into the atmosphere and can cause a complete
spiritual shift that can be felt in the physical realm.
Worshipping God can be an emotional experience. If it
becomes emotional, I encourage you to embrace it as a time
of release. Tears represent unspoken matters of the heart.
Allowing yourself to become vulnerable with God is another
act of worship that impacts the atmosphere.

TODAY'S DECLARATION

I worship You, Lord, with gladness; I come before You with
joyful songs.

27

DAY 8

Sister Talk & Reflection

You have the spiritual authority to change the atmosphere of the room your Little One is in so that it is a place of worship. I challenge you to have a conversation with the room where your Little One is, then write about what you experienced. Tell the space what you do and do not like. Tell it what is and what will be, even if all you do is repeat your declaration.

_____

_____

_____

_____

_____

_____

_____

_____

_____

_____

_____

WHAT'S ON MY HEART & MIND

PRAYERS

_____

_____

_____

_____

_____

_____

_____

_____

_____

_____

_____

_____

_____

_____

_____

_____

_____

_____

_____

_____

DAY 9

Keeping the Secret

*Again, truly I tell you that if two of you on earth
agree about anything they ask for, it will be done
for them by my Father in heaven. For where two or
three gather in my name, there am I with them*
(MATTHEW 18:19–20).

As you are believing for the progression and healing of your
Little One, you will have to fight to stay in a positive mindset
at times. Even right now, you may not feel like quoting
Scriptures, singing a song, or being in faith. You want to
have the right to be in your feelings and speak your real
thoughts. In times like these, you need an ally. For me, that
was my sister. I knew I could say exactly how I felt, let my
tears fall, or complain, and she would reel me back in. She
was my compass—always able to point me back to North
(in this case, to God). It is important to have your secret
keeper—the person/people who you know will pray for you
when you can't pray for yourself.

I call this person a secret keeper because they will not share
your sentiments and moments of fear and doubt. They
understand that you only want to sow seeds of faith, and
your secret keeper won't allow you to have a prolonged

period of negative talk. This person can be your significant other, a sibling, a relative, a friend, a spiritual leader, etc. Regardless of the relation, they are willing to present your cares to God when the load seems too heavy for you to carry. Your secret keeper *does not* replace God; they go to Him on your behalf. Honestly, at times, we want a physical person that can understand us, hear us, and respond. God can use your secret keeper to minister to you if you remain open-hearted.

Your secret keeper shouldn't replace your significant other either. Although my secret keeper was my sister, Joshua understood that she could relate to me as a mother in a way he could not. I would summarize our conversations with him because I wanted him to gauge my self-awareness while supporting me. Together, the two of them kept me focused because I refused to become depressed. Spiritual service announcement: Birthing a premature Little One does not mean you will inevitably experience postpartum depression! Your secret keeper can help you steer clear of it as you confide in them. This is a major reason why having one or more confidants is vital. You can unload your frustrations and cares and keep going.

If you happen to be in a battle with depression, we—God, your support system, and me!—are here for you just the same. Postpartum depression is a unique experience for each mother in the fight but with some shared commonalities. I had to fight daily, and to be honest, although I've written this devotional, I still strive to maintain my mental stability.

I understand that, at times, the pressures of life may seem all-consuming with no way out; however, with God, there is *always* a healthy way out! He is the way maker! The trust we talked about in the previous devo entry is extremely necessary. Trust God just like you trust the chair you're sitting in right now. My example may seem like a stretch, but trusting Him can become just as easy.

In the moments when uncertainty creeps in and the weight of your current circumstance seems too much to handle, call on your secret keeper. When you join in prayer and faith with your secret keeper, you are welcoming God into the situation. The bond that has been created through mutual agreement about the health of your baby continues even when you cannot hold up your end. Your faith has already been put in motion, and your secret keeper will help lift your burdens.

HIS PROMISES

> *"My intercessor is my friend as my eyes pour*
> *out tears to God; on behalf of a man he pleads*
> *with God as one pleads for a friend"*
> (JOB 16:20–21).

As you know, my sister was my intercessor. She went before God on my behalf when I didn't have the words or the strength to do it myself. Whoever you choose as your secret keeper can do the same for you. They can literally share your heart's sentiments with God. It is such a blessing that God has made room for someone to go to Him on our behalf.

> *"Therefore encourage one another and build each*
> *other up, just as in fact you are doing"*
> (1 THESSALONIANS 5:11).

You will need to give your secret keeper permission to encourage you even when you don't want to hear it. They will be sensitive to your needs while also discerning when to be a listening ear and when to help guide you back to a place of faith. You may be required to yield so that you can take in the tough pills of truth. Know that these are prescribed to you in love.

TODAY'S DECLARATION

When my Secret Keeper and I agree about anything we ask for, it will be done for us by You in heaven. For where two or three gather in Your name, there You are with us. (See Matthew 18:20.)

DAY 10

Sister Talk & Reflection

It's important to have someone to confide in and help you stay in the faith lane. Who can you choose as your secret keeper? Have a conversation with them about the role you want them to play and why you chose them. Share your secret keeper and their strengths below. List the items you want them to agree about with you in prayer. How can sharing with your secret keeper help you remain joyful and avoid depression?

_____

_____

_____

_____

_____

_____

_____

_____

_____

_____

WHAT'S ON MY HEART & MIND

PRAYERS

DAY 11

Their Time vs. His Time

Truly I tell you, if anyone says to this mountain,
"Go, throw yourself in the sea," and does not
doubt in their heart but believes that what they
say will happen, it will be done for them
(MARK 11:23).

When Caleb was born, I was told he would likely be in the hospital until he was full term. This meant his stay would be about eight weeks. I refused to accept that as the truth. I prayed about everything the medical staff told me. Although they said eight weeks, I thanked God in advance for allowing Caleb to come home sooner. Sis, you have the power and authority to speak things into existence! There is a difference between *their* timing and *God's* timing; however, in some instances, the two align. But I'm specifically referring to the times when what is shared doesn't sit well with you and doesn't register with your spirit.

Just as you are being spiritually equipped to make a change, I hope you are being equipped to do the same in the natural realm. Naturally speaking, you know your Little One best. You are learning about their likes, dislikes, and needs as you are spending time together. Use what you are learning and advocate for what is best for your Little One. This may be a challenge if you are a quiet and laid-back person. If this describes you, I encourage you to allow God to empower you to speak up on behalf of your Little One. You are not insulting the medical staff's ability. You are saying what your Little One is unable to say. At times, I had to tell the medical staff about what Caleb needed despite their opinion. I had to do so repeatedly until they took what I said into consideration. When they adhered to my request, Caleb began to improve. Yes, they have medical degrees, but you are your Little One's mother!

What seems to be in front of you does not have to remain that way. I got tired of seeing Caleb with a tube in his nose, another down this throat, and a monitor on his foot. The oxygen machine and feeding tubes became like the mountains Jesus said we could speak to and they would be removed (Mark 11:23). I spoke to those devices and told them they had to go. I shared the mountains with my secret keeper so she could pray in agreement with my proclamation. I told Joshua my desire, and he stood with me. One day, we walked into Caleb's room to find one tube was gone, and then the other! When this happened, I thanked God, but I didn't stop speaking God's promises. I transitioned my prayers to the list of things I was grateful for.

HIS PROMISES

*"Finally, brothers and sisters, whatever is true,
whatever is noble, whatever is right, whatever is pure,
whatever is lovely, whatever is admirable-if anything is
excellent or praiseworthy-think about such things"*
(PHILIPPIANS 4:8).

A time may come when you hear news that you don't like. Try not to take it personally. When you do, you open yourself up to placing blame. The blame can seep into our actions, and we must be careful of what we say to those caring for our Little One. Many times, I wanted to share choice words with the medical staff because of what was said to me. Suddenly, God would remind me that Caleb is His first and that He was taking care of the situation. All I had to do was stay in my place of faith. Easier said than done, but I know you can do it.

*"Now faith is confidence in what we hope for
and assurance about what we do not see"*
(HEBREWS 11:1).

The concept of faith has been woven throughout each entry. I want you to remember what faith is, according to Scripture. Having faith doesn't equate to an easy journey, especially when our natural inclination is to believe what we can see. I understand you may be discouraged by the length of time your Little One is in the hospital. You may feel as if the circumstances you are facing aren't changing fast enough. Try not to fret. Instead, unleash your faith and allow it to bring what you're hoping for to fruition.

TODAY'S DECLARATION

I say to (your mountain), be gone! Go throw yourself in the sea. I do not doubt in my heart, and I believe what I say will happen, so it will be done for me and my Little One!

DAY 12

Wins, Answers to prayers, & Victories

When you are believing for something different from the doctor's report, you need a focused mindset. Philippians 4:8 lists what you should focus on. What are some of the right, lovely, and praiseworthy things you can think on? How does changing your thoughts positively affect your journey?

_____

_____

_____

_____

_____

_____

_____

_____

_____

_____

_____

_____

WHAT'S ON MY HEART & MIND

_____

_____

_____

_____

_____

_____

_____

_____

_____

_____

_____

_____

_____

_____

_____

_____

_____

_____

_____

WINS, ANSWERS TO PRAYERS, & VICTORIES

_____

_____

_____

_____

_____

_____

_____

_____

_____

_____

_____

_____

_____

_____

_____

_____

_____

_____

_____

_____

DAY 13

Having a Listening Ear

So faith comes from hearing,
and hearing by the word of Christ
(ROMANS 10:17).

During the time of believing the best for your Little One, you are seeking God and speaking your declaration as a means to build yourself up.

As you hear the words you are speaking, you allow them to take root within you. On Day 12, I shared that Caleb's tubes were removed. I had to remember how God moved on our behalf in order to fuel my faith as I was believing for even greater outcomes. That victory was the motivation I needed to continue believing and seeing beyond natural circumstances. I titled this entry "Having A Listening Ear" because our faith increases as we hear God's Word. In my case, I heard His word each time I declared *His promises* over Caleb.

Think about the times you heard a song repeatedly. Eventually, you started singing it in your head, and you could even visualize what you were hearing. The same can happen with your declarations. As you continue to speak your declarations, free yourself to see what you're using the Scriptures to believe for. Practicing this is the equivalent of developing a spiritual vision board. As a matter of fact, you can use your declarations to create your personal vision board! Developing this can be a collective activity that keeps you connected to your support system. (We will talk more about this in the next entry.) The vision board is an option and an alternative way to practice and support your faith. As your schedule is busy, it's completely understandable if you can't create one right now. If you can, great! If not, no pressure; mental visualization works just as well.

HIS PROMISES

"Devote yourselves to prayer, being watchful and thankful"
(COLOSSIANS 4:2).

I have shared a lot about prayer, and I can't emphasize its importance enough. This verse from Colossians encourages you to stay the course by committing to prayer while maintaining a spirit of expectancy and gratefulness.

"Therefore I tell you, whatever you ask for in prayer,
believe that you have received it, and it will be yours"
(MARK 11:24).

When you pray and declare, you are speaking into existence what isn't before your natural eyes as if it already is. The word "received" is mentioned in the past tense, meaning something that already happened. What you say will become what you see in your mind and eventually what you see with your eyes.

TODAY'S DECLARATION

I have asked for (your request) in prayer. I believe that I have received it and it is mine.

DAY 14

As you are believing God for the answer to your prayers, I challenge you to practice visualizing what you're believing for. Take some time to mediate on it. If you need help, do an online search for an image that relates to what you are hoping for. Look at the image repeatedly. Use the space below to write out what you see. You can even use the space to draw a picture.

_____

_____

_____

_____

_____

_____

_____

_____

_____

_____

_____

WHAT'S ON MY HEART & MIND

PRAYERS

DAY 15

Maintaining Relationships

*A friend loves at all times, and a brother
is born for a time of adversity*
(PROVERBS 17:17).

Having a Little One in the hospital for any length of time can be very overwhelming. You spend a great deal of time at the hospital in almost a routine fashion. Although you are focused on taking care of your Little One, the demands of life unfortunately continue to exist.

Joshua and I had to make arrangements with our jobs because of how unexpected Caleb's arrival was. So many people were calling and texting us for updates. Many people wanted to visit Caleb, and we never heard from others. I found myself becoming distant and not really wanting to talk to anyone because I didn't want to answer any more questions. I had to realize that people were reaching out because they cared. To be honest, we needed to be on the receiving end of their love. We needed a friend to come by and bring us dinner because we hadn't eaten and were too tired to cook. I needed the occasional funny text to help me refocus.

You need to remain connected to those who are important to you. Allow your friends and family to play the role God has positioned them for. At times, you might expect certain things from specific people, then become upset when you don't get them. I've been there. When we react like that, we are limiting God. He has strategically placed people in our lives for specific reasons at divine times. This includes your significant other. He will be there for you if you allow him to be. It may sound like I am being presumptuous; however, I am saying that there is something he can do. What he can do and what you want him to do for you and your Little One could potentially be two different things. Through it all, remember to trust God wholeheartedly and maintain your relationship with Him.

HIS PROMISES

"I long to see you that I may impart to you some spiritual gift to make you strong that is, that you and I may be mutually encouraged by each other's faith"
(ROMANS 1:11–12).

On Day 10, you identified your secret keeper(s) as the one(s) you confide in during the times you need to vent or be redirected. Keep in mind, those outside of the secret keeper role are just as instrumental. My relationship with my mom grew deeper than I ever thought possible. She was the pleasant and consistent one that I needed and looked forward to having at the hospital almost every day. Out of the many days Caleb was in the hospital, my mom only missed two. Others supported us physically, monetarily, and spiritually. Maintaining relationships during trying times can make way for deeper and more intimate connections with the family and friends in your village. As you meet and talk to other mothers and families in the hospital, new friendships can develop. In addition, you can sharpen one another's faith.

> *"Fear not, I am with you; be not dismayed for I am your God; I will strengthen you, I will help you, I will uphold you with my righteous right hand"*
> (ISAIAH 41:10).

This is such a wonderful promise from our God. What I love is that He doesn't simply tell us not to fear, but He shares several reasons why not to. Allow Him to be your strength and help. Allow Him to lift you up when you are down. Sis, I hope that you can sense the magnitude of His care for you in this verse.

TODAY'S DECLARATION

My friends and family always love me, and they are there for me in times of difficulty.

DAY 16

Sister Talk & Reflection

Staying connected to the important people in your life can be difficult, but it is essential. Describe how you can allow your family and friends to care for and express their love to you.

_____

_____

_____

_____

_____

_____

_____

_____

_____

_____

_____

_____

WHAT'S ON MY HEART & MIND

PRAYERS

_____

_____

_____

_____

_____

_____

_____

_____

_____

_____

_____

_____

_____

_____

_____

_____

_____

_____

_____

_____

_____

DAY 17

Self-Care

*Dear friend, I pray that you may enjoy good
health and that all may go well with you,
even as your soul is getting along well*
(3 JOHN 1:2).

Sis, it is essential that you take care of yourself first so that
you can be in good health and care for your Little One.
A lack of self-care opens the door wide for the enemy to
wear you down emotionally and mentally. To be honest,
I struggled in this area and from time to time, I still do. I
tried my best not to feel guilty for sleeping a little longer
than usual before going to the hospital. Mom-guilt caused
me to go against my doctor's orders as I drove to the hospital
even though they told me not to drive because it would put
a strain on the C-section incision area. Because I didn't rest,
listen, or wait until Joshua was off work to drive me, I had a
hard time walking and holding Caleb. I share this with you
to help you see how you do have to put yourself first in order
to have a better outcome. In my case, good health would've
allowed me to have better quality time with Caleb.

Another aspect of self-care is patience. You already know
you need patience while your Little One is in the hospital,

but you also need patience with yourself. It is not selfish to take time to relax in your own way. You must remember that your body is still healing and recovering from labor. I want to encourage you to identify your self-care needs as well as the practices that could result in fatigue. Do your best to avoid activities and habits that will tire you out. If you choose to take on a task, try sharing it with your support system. Your support system can help you by ensuring you're not taking on too much and by encouraging you to set aside time for yourself so that you can reset and be completely available for your Little One.

Being in a healthy place mentally, spiritually, emotionally, and physically is crucial to being fully present with your Little One. Lack in any area can negatively impact your faith walk and the time you spend with your Little One. Remember that self-care isn't reserved for when you feel as if you are on the verge of a breakdown. Practicing self-care means taking care of yourself consistently and checking in with those around you, especially your significant other, to let them know your needs.

HIS PROMISES

> *"Come to me, all you who are weary and*
> *burdened, and I will give you rest"*
> (MATTHEW 11:28).

God is there for you, and you can cast your concerns and burden upon Him. He doesn't want you to be overwhelmed, but rather He wants you to be free to worship and believe Him for your Little One's needs. Rest is more than going to sleep and is deeper than self-care. Rest is about submitting to God, relaxing in Him, and knowing He has your back.

"Cast all your anxiety on him because he cares for you."
(1 PETER 5:7).

Release your cares and let Him care for you. When you take your hands off your worries and release them to God, you allow God to do what He does best: be God. When you hold on to your concerns, it's almost as if you're saying to God that you can take care of them better than He can. He loves you so much that He wants you to give *all* your anxiety and cares to Him.

TODAY'S DECLARATION

I am in good health and all is well with me, even as all is well with my soul.

DAY 18

Wins, Answers to prayers, & Victories

As a mother, you spend so much time taking care of your Little One and others around you. It is time to take care of yourself. Make a list of the ways you can communicate what you need in order to take care of you. Share your list with your significant other and those close to you.

_____

_____

_____

_____

_____

_____

_____

_____

_____

_____

_____

_____

_____

WHAT'S ON MY HEART & MIND

WINS, ANSWERS TO PRAYERS, & VICTORIES

_____

_____

_____

_____

_____

_____

_____

_____

_____

_____

_____

_____

_____

_____

_____

_____

_____

_____

_____

_____

_____

DAY 19

When Things Don't Go as Planned

*And we know that in all things God works
for the good of those who love him, who have
been called according to his purpose*
(ROMANS 8:28).

At one point during Caleb's time in the hospital, he was progressing so well that it was time for him to take the various tests needed for him to go home. Caleb passed all the tests! I was excited and relieved! Joshua and I made all the necessary preparations for him to come home. We told our family and friends that Caleb would soon be released. Hours before it was time for us to pick him up, I received a call saying that Caleb had a major alarm and he would be unable to come home. I lost it emotionally, and for a moment, spiritually. I was driving at the time. It took everything I had to make it home. All I kept saying to God was that I wanted my baby home with me. Once I arrived home and walked into our bedroom, I broke down. I told Joshua what the nurse said. Caleb wasn't coming home. I gave myself permission to feel every emotion that filled my soul. I was hurt, angry, and scared all at the same time. I couldn't image my son's little body continuing to endure the physical challenges and alarms.

After I expressed all the emotions I was feeling, I had to remember that Caleb was God's first. It wasn't enough to remember this fact in my mind. No, I began to say it out loud repeatedly. I needed to believe it again! I had to intentionally activate my faith because I knew God wasn't done working. This was a challenge, to say the least, but I gathered my scattered thoughts and put my faith to work.

HIS PROMISES

"As the heavens are higher than the earth, so are my ways higher than your ways and my thoughts than your thoughts" (ISAIAH 55:9).

It can be difficult to accept a report you don't want to hear. Your faith will be called into question. But now isn't the time to give up. Now is the time to remember that you don't know everything that's in the works. In my case, it was better for Caleb to stay in the hospital instead of coming home, have an alarming experience, and not be connected to a machine. We would have no idea he needed help, and we wouldn't know what to do. I know it's difficult to think optimistically in the midst of a challenge, but keep believing, keep on pushing, and don't give up!

"Being confident of this, that he who began a good work in you will carry it on to completion until the day of Christ Jesus" (PHILIPPIANS 1:6).

When things don't go according to our plans, we have to remember whose plans are greater. Getting to the place of acceptance can take some time. This Scripture is essential to keep in mind. God promises to finish what He started. *The good work in you* is the work of faith. It is your faith that carries you and helps you make it. It is the spiritual tenacity that does not allow you to give up.

TODAY'S DECLARATION

All things are working together for my good and the good of (my Little One) because I love You and I am called according to Your purpose.

DAY 20

Sister Talk & Reflection

Typically, you write in this section, but I want you to do something new. Take some time to saturate yourself in a faith-boosting activity. This may be listening to music, reading, watching a sermon, going for a walk, etc. If you desire to use the space below, simply record the activity you plan to engage in, and then enjoy it!

WHAT'S ON MY HEART & MIND

PRAYERS

DAY 21

Cheerleaders

> *Do not be anxious about anything, but in*
> *every situation, by prayer and petition, with*
> *thanksgiving, present your requests to God*
> (PHILIPPIANS 4:6).

After dealing with not being able to take Caleb home, I felt as if I needed to regroup and reset. I realized I needed more concentrated spiritual support. I sent a group text to key family members who were believers, and I asked them to refrain from asking questions about when Caleb was coming home but to believe with us that he was coming home soon. I asked them to not ask because I never wanted to have to explain why my son wasn't home like I said he would be. I let them know I would share updates as we felt necessary, and I asked them to focus on praying for Caleb. I named the group text, Caleb's Cheerleaders. My family was cheering on Caleb in faith.

This entry is separate from the entries on "Secret Keepers and Maintaining Relationships" because this team of believers was specifically for Caleb. My Secret Keeper was for me, and our relationships with our family and friends were for us as a family. Caleb's Cheerleaders were on the front line with us, standing in faith that we would receive Caleb's release home. We thanked God every day for Caleb being home even though we saw him in the hospital. We had too many victories to believe otherwise. You don't have to wait for a turn of events to identify your cheerleaders. You can rally your cheerleaders together whenever you deem necessary.

I created this devotional for you, knowing that trials would arise, and I want to provide you with strategies and support. I know you don't want to hear anyone else say, "Don't worry, everything will be okay," but sis, I'm joining the team in a sense. I'm encouraging you not to worry, but the fact is, we all worry. Your Little One is in the hospital, so of course, you will worry. But don't allow worry to consume you. You have your secret keeper and now your cheerleaders to share your sentiments and burdens with. After unloading, go to God and share your heart with Him. Then thank Him, and tell your cheerleaders how they can agree with you in prayer.

HIS PROMISES

"I urge, then, first of all, that petitions, prayers, intercession and thanksgiving be made for all people"
(1 TIMOTHY 2:1).

Instructions are given in this Scripture. Your cheerleaders are a part of "all people." Welcome them into the role of intercessor. This Scripture sums up the purpose of your cheerleaders. They are cheering and believing the best for your Little One at all times.

"Praise be to the God and Father of our Lord Jesus Christ, the Father of compassion and the God of all comfort, who comforts us in all our troubles, so that we can comfort those in any trouble with the comfort we ourselves receive from God"
(2 CORINTHIANS 1:3–4).

Your cheerleaders can serve you because they have received strength and comfort from God. They give out of their own supply. This is a Scripture to share with them as a reminder to stay connected to the source. At the same time, this verse provides assurance to you as to how they can be there for you.

TODAY'S DECLARATION

I am not anxious about anything, and I will pray and petition You with thanksgiving.

DAY 22

Sister Talk & Reflection

It can be helpful to have an inner circle of people—
cheerleaders—who are focused on supporting your Little
One. Who will you ask to rally alongside you in prayer?
Describe how they will cheer for your Little One.

_____

_____

_____

_____

_____

_____

_____

_____

_____

_____

_____

_____

_____

_____

WHAT'S ON MY HEART & MIND

PRAYERS

_____

_____

_____

_____

_____

_____

_____

_____

_____

_____

_____

_____

_____

_____

_____

_____

_____

_____

_____

DAY 23

Preparing for Homecoming Day

*And my God will meet all your needs according
to the riches of his glory in Christ Jesus*
(PHILIPPIANS 4:19).

We were finally given the green light for Caleb to come
home. We only told a select few friends because we didn't
want them to show up at the hospital, thinking we were still
there. We went to the extent of sanitizing and thoroughly
cleaning every space where Caleb could potentially spend
time at home. Joshua and I made sure we had everything we
needed for Caleb. Or so we thought.

We were so focused on what was tangible that the spiritual
things were neglected. Hours before we left home to get
Caleb, I remembered Caleb was God's first and he was a
gift to us. I went into Caleb's room and blessed his room
in prayer. I thanked God for everything that He blessed us
with for the caring of Caleb. I thanked Him for answering
our prayers concerning Caleb. Then I walked through the
rest of the house, blessing each room and expressing my
gratitude. I fought feelings of guilt. How could I forget
about God in that moment? I knew the human fault factor
(we all fall short at times); however, it was a reality check

about how quickly I could forget Who was making this possible.

Preparing for your Little One to come home is more about your spiritual preparation than the physical preparation. To be more specific, when you continue maintaining your spiritual relationship with God, you are more equipped to handle all that may occur after you bring your Little One home.

HIS PROMISES

"When you enter a house, first say, 'Peace to this house."
(LUKE 10:5).

This may seem like an odd Scripture to use in this entry; however, maintaining peace is so important. You and your Little One are connected, and they can pick up on your feelings. Peace is something you possess and exude. Having an atmosphere of peace nurtures a peaceful Little One.

"For I know the plans I have for you, "plans to prosper you and not to harm you, plans to give you hope and a future"
(JEREMIAH 29:11).

As you prepare for your Little One's homecoming, you may realize that you don't have everything you think you need physically or spiritually. I want you to know that it is okay.

I'm telling you this confidently because God has a plan for you, just as His Word states. He will make a way for you to have what you need if you remain open to receiving it. Utilize your support system. Remember to tap into your resources as well (Scriptures, music, videos, websites to organizations, links to sale items, etc.).

TODAY'S DECLARATION

As recorded in Your Word, You will meet all of our needs according to the riches of Your glory in Christ Jesus. (See Philippians 4:19.)

DAY 24

Wins, Answers to prayers, & Victories

Your Little One's homecoming day is as much about being spiritually prepared as it is about being prepared with baby items. Share how you plan to prepare your home and heart for your Little One.

_____

_____

_____

_____

_____

_____

_____

_____

_____

_____

_____

_____

_____

WHAT'S ON MY HEART & MIND

WINS, ANSWERS TO PRAYERS, & VICTORIES

_____

_____

_____

_____

_____

_____

_____

_____

_____

_____

_____

_____

_____

_____

_____

_____

_____

_____

_____

_____

_____

DAY 25

Eliminating Expectations

Now to him who is able to do immeasurably more than all we ask or imagine, according to his power that is at work within us (EPHESIANS 3:20).

Having Caleb home was a dream come true! I was overcome with emotions. Our prayers had been answered. Caleb was not only home, but he was home before the doctors said he would be. Joshua and I often looked at each other, smiled, and said, "He's finally home." I was honored to be his mother, and I was in awe of him.

A few days after settling in, we had to create a routine. We needed to make major adjustments. Caleb continued his hospital schedule of sleeping and eating. This meant we needed to align our lifestyle with his. I didn't think about this during my preparation time. His schedule placed a huge demand on me, and I quickly became overwhelmed. I counted the hours of sleep I didn't get and how many other responsibilities were piling up. I counted how many times bottles needed to be washed, loads of laundry that needed to be done, and the number of diapers I changed. I couldn't believe the number of people who told me to sleep while he slept. Yeah, right. I eventually learned that I was not

Superwoman and I didn't have to strive to be. What I can do one day doesn't determine what I can do the next. When I needed help, I had to let someone know.

Joshua was amazing through it all. I quickly learned that communicating my needs and being specific was the best way to get the help I needed from him. I want to encourage you to lighten the expectations you have on yourself. You won't get things right every day and it is okay. Utilize the support you have, starting with those in your home.

Rest is an important component of eliminating expectations. As I shared before, rest is not just about getting sleep. Rest is a self-release and a self-assurance in God. It is activated by your faith and upheld by His peace. Resting allows God to take care of you. We previously addressed self-care and what you can do to take care of yourself. Now, I'm referring to God orchestrating things to make them easier for you to be a mother, significant other, and to fulfill any other role you may have.

HIS PROMISES

> *"I sought the Lord, and he answered me;*
> *he delivered me from all my fears"*
> (PSALM 34:4).

Your first support, even if there seems to be no one else, is God. Give Him the expectations you placed on yourself and talk to Him about how you are feeling regarding others' expectations of you. Know that He cares for you so much that He wants to know the details of your feelings.

> *"When anxiety was great within me, your*
> *consolation brought me joy"*
> (PSALM 94:19).

When you give God the cares that overwhelm and burden you, you receive rest in return. Rest also makes way for God's revelation. Through revelation, God can share with you how what burdened you can be prevented. He won't stop there; He will also give you confirmation and reminders to help you avoid future burdens and possible burnout.

TODAY'S DECLARATION

You are able to do more than I can ask or think. (See Ephesians 3:20.)

DAY 26

Sister Talk & Reflection

A significant demand falls on mothers of premature Little Ones. What are some of the expectations placed on you? How will you communicate when you need help, and who will you call on?

_____

_____

_____

_____

_____

_____

_____

_____

_____

_____

_____

_____

_____

_____

WHAT'S ON MY HEART & MIND

_____

_____

_____

_____

_____

_____

_____

_____

_____

_____

_____

_____

_____

_____

_____

_____

_____

_____

_____

_____

_____

PRAYERS

_____

_____

_____

_____

_____

_____

_____

_____

_____

_____

_____

_____

_____

_____

_____

_____

_____

_____

_____

_____

_____

DAY 27

God's Got Your Back

*And he said unto me, My grace is sufficient for thee:
for my strength is made perfect in weakness*
(2 CORINTHIANS 12:9).

Being a mother is such an honor and privilege. Just think, God entrusted you with one of His invaluable treasures. At times, I would stare at Caleb in total awe while he was sleeping. I will always be grateful to God for blessing me with an amazing son. As awesome as this privilege is, there were—and still are—days when I felt like I couldn't handle or do certain things, but God showed me I could accomplish the task at hand. He gave me supernatural grace to "run my race." Consider grace as God's strength and ability empowering you to do what you cannot do in your own might. As a result of receiving His grace, I thanked God daily. I didn't just *know* His grace was available to me. I experienced it personally, and I believe you can too. I allowed God to parent with me. The load became easier, and I eventually stopped second-guessing myself. I allowed myself to partake of the peace that I had declared in our home.

Caleb had a specific feeding regime, and I not only had to remember it, I had to teach it to those helping us care for

Caleb. We were blessed that my mother took care of him while Joshua and I returned to work. I had to accept God's grace in letting go and allowing God to step in again through my mom. I trusted her, and I knew she loved Caleb, but a part of me was nervous. Step in, God did. My mom began to send updates, pictures, and videos throughout the day, which were very reassuring. As your Little One is home or will be home soon, I want to remind you that God has your back.

HIS PROMISES

> *"The Lord gives strength to is people; the Lord blesses his people with peace"*
> (PSALM 29:11).

Thank God for the strength to be the best mother you can be, understanding that there's no ruler to measure you against. Accept that you are doing the best you can with what you have. This can help you remain in a place of peace just as you continue to declare your home is.

> *"And God is able to bless you abundantly, so that in all things at all times, having all that you need, you will abound in every good work"*
> (2 CORINTHIANS 9:8).

God is willing and able to bless you! He can bless you to the point that you have all you need. I'm not sharing this with you just to make you feel good. The Word of God says it! "Abound" means to prosper. Sis, we know worrying happens. Do what it takes to make worry temporary by leaning on the truth in this Scripture. Part of the good work mentioned here is the good work of being a mother.

TODAY'S DECLARATION

Your grace is sufficient for me. Your strength is made perfect in my weakness. (See 2 Corinthians 12:9.)

DAY 28

Sister Talk & Reflection

God's grace is enough for you even when you are weak. His strength is made perfect. Reflect on a time when you needed God's strength and how God graced you with it. Record your experience below.

_____

_____

_____

_____

_____

_____

_____

_____

_____

_____

_____

_____

_____

WHAT'S ON MY HEART & MIND

PRAYERS

_____

_____

_____

_____

_____

_____

_____

_____

_____

_____

_____

_____

_____

_____

_____

_____

_____

_____

_____

_____

_____

_____

DAY 29

*And let us consider how we may spur one
another on toward love and good deeds*
(HEBREWS 10:24).

I pray that you've experienced the generosity of your village
while reading this devotional. Maybe you have received
food, money, or items for your Little One. I am sure that
you've thanked those who have been a blessing in any way. I
challenge you to be a blessing to others by sowing into their
lives. Sowing isn't a difficult concept. It can happen in the
form of words of encouragement over the phone, in person,
email, text, or a card. Do you know a mother that is going
through something similar to what you've overcome? Share
a testimony with her of how God was with you and carried
you through. Your words can revitalize and strengthen
others. You can sow into your significant other and let him
know what a great support he is to you and how much you
appreciate him. You can sow into your Little One by sharing
Scriptures about who they are and by sharing God's purpose
for their lives.

Sowing seeds in good ground yields a harvest. Yes, harvesting
is great, but the purpose of this entry is to demonstrate

another way to thank God for who He is and all He has done. As a receiver of God's goodness, sow into others because of what God has given you. This concept is akin to the domino effect. Sowing into someone's life can cause a chain reaction that impacts many lives in a major way.

When you sow into others' lives, you are paying it forward. You might never know the impact you will have on someone's life, but know you are making a positive difference!

HIS PROMISES

"Now he who supplies seed to the sower and bread for food will also supply and increase your store of seed and will enlarge the harvest of righteousness"
(2 CORINTHIANS 9:10).

You don't have to be concerned about whether you'll have what you need in order to sow because God has already taken care of that. He has taken care of it so much so that, not only will He give you the seed to sow, but He will replace it and give you an increase (harvest).

"Give, and it will be given to you. A good measure, pressed down, shaken together and running over, will be poured into your lap. For with the measure you use, it will be measured to you"
(LUKE 6:38).

When you give, you make room for more. You make room for more to give. As you continue to practice giving, you are developing a lifestyle. Think about how amazing it would be to live a life of perpetual blessings!

TODAY'S DECLARATION

I will consider how I can encourage others to love and do good deeds.

DAY 30

Wins, Answers to prayers, & Victories

When you sow, you are blessing someone else. Sowing is a demonstration of how grateful you are for what God has given you. Think about the many ways seeds have been sown into your life and the life of your family while going through the process of caring for a premature Little One. Describe how you can be a sower that encourages others in love.

_____

_____

_____

_____

_____

_____

_____

_____

_____

_____

_____

_____

WHAT'S ON MY HEART & MIND

WINS, ANSWERS TO PRAYERS, & VICTORIES

DAY 31

You're His First Too

*See what great love the Father has lavished
on us, the we should be called children
of God! And that is what we are!*
(1 JOHN 3:1).

You've made it to the final devo entry, and you have not
been forgotten. I want to celebrate you! Whether or not
someone has told you this, I want you to know that you are
amazing! There's not another mother like you. As a mother,
you have a special type of endurance and resiliency that is
unspeakable. I want to thank you for being the wonderfully
unique mother you are.

I titled this entry 'You're His First Too' because I want you to
firmly embrace this truth. You started out as a baby just like
your Little One. You are a gift too. Yes, you have matured
into a beautiful woman, but to God, you're still His Little
One. He has not forgotten about you, sis. He wants His Little
One (you) to know that He appreciates you for allowing
Him to be God in your Little One's life and for doing all
that you have done. Your Heavenly Father celebrates you and
loves you immensely.

God has adorned you with His love. He wants you to wear it proudly because He is so very proud of you. He is grateful that you accepted the calling to be the mother of your Little One. You are designed for this role for such a time as this!

TODAY'S DECLARATION

What great love You have lavished on me, that I am called a child of God! (See 1 John 3:1.) And that is what I am!

SISTER TALK & REFLECTION

Think about the ways that you can celebrate yourself. Now go and do them! You deserve it, Sis!

Closing Letter to My Sister

Hey Sis,

I am proud of you for taking on the challenge of completing this devotional. I thank you for being vulnerable and committed enough to allow God to move in your heart, life, and on your Little One's behalf. My prayer is that as you journeyed through the thirty-one days, your faith blossomed. I also pray that you are empowered and encouraged. Most importantly, I hope and pray that you believe that your Little One is God's first, and so are you!

This devotional is yours. Go back and reread the encouragement days and reflection days as often as you need to. If you need more space to write, use a journal or any other form of documentation that best suits you. Regardless of the format, take God with you.

I would love to hear about you, your Little One, and your journey experience with this devotional. Take a moment to share a review on Amazon. You can contact me via email, and we can connect on social media. I look forward to meeting and hearing from you!

I also invite you to join our online community of Sisters at *byusisters.buildyouup.org*.

Your sister in love,
Jamie
Email: *byusisters@gmail.com*
Instagram & Facebook: @byusisters

HEART PAGES

HEART PAGES

HEART PAGES

_____

_____

_____

_____

_____

_____

_____

_____

_____

_____

_____

_____

_____

_____

_____

_____

_____

_____

_____

_____

_____

_____

HEART PAGES

HEART PAGES

HEART PAGES

_____

_____

_____

_____

_____

_____

_____

_____

_____

_____

_____

_____

_____

_____

_____

_____

_____

_____

_____

_____

_____

_____

_____

Acknowledgments

I dedicate this book to God. This is His book and His message. I give it back just like Hannah swore to God that she would give her son Samuel back to Him. There aren't enough words in any language that would allow me to fully express how I feel about God and what He has done from the time of Caleb's birth to the very writing of this book. I am truly unable to do anything without Him. Thank you, Daddy!

To my love, Joshua: You are an incredible partner. You are my prayers answered! You have been a support in ways you don't even know, from your words of wisdom to the jokes you make. We experienced a series of ups and downs as we endured the journey to Caleb's homecoming day, yet you were encouraging, you dealt with my emotions, you helped me cope with physical pain, you sacrificed your sleep, and you made yourself of service to me. You are amazing! The love you have for our son often leaves me speechless; the bond between the two of you is unbreakable. Caleb lights up when you walk in the room and when he hears your voice. Thank you for allowing me to tell our story in order to help others.

To my nephew, Dawson: You are a part of my heart and will never leave. I love you. I learned so much about you while your mother and I were pregnant at the same time. You gave me hope! I never had the chance to hold you in my arms, yet I hold you within my heart. I thank you for being with Caleb every day and for loving your brother-cousin. Thank you for being a light for your mother and your father. Thank you for being the one that continues to tell them to keep going, knowing that you, too, belong to God first. Dawson James Donald McQueen, you are love, and you are loved!

To my son, my first born, my lovey, Caleb Troy Townes: You are a perfect example of God's love made manifest. I say that because you have defied the odds. You are a walking miracle. You are God's promise and His truth before our eyes every single day. Thank you for being the light that you are. You shine so bright. I thank God that it will never go away. You are a blessing to all that you encounter. You are loved everywhere that you go, and you are already one who makes an impact and causes change. Thank you for changing me! I am a better woman because of you. The meaning of your name—*faithful* and *strong-willed*—holds power. Walk in it boldly, son. I love you forever and ever!

To Caleb's Cheerleaders: Thank you for loving us and for being such a blessing to us as intercessors. God truly used our group text to knit us closer as a family. We went from talking occasionally to sharing almost daily, even now. I pray it continues. I love you all!

To my Secret Keeper, Monica: A special thank you. You are who people dream of having as a sister and best friend. I am blessed to be able to say you are both to me. Thank you for

ACKNOWLEDGMENTS

loving me unconditionally and for being the one to help me refocus and remember that I ascend when I surrender.

To the Truth2RenewHearts Publishing team: Thank you. Writing this book while I was processing my journey was not easy, but you helped me and made my dream attainable. I thank God for giving you the ability to help authors fulfill their mission and purpose in a loving, safe, and professional manner.

Thank you to everyone who prayed for us and supported us through our journey!

About the Author

JAMIE C. JOHNSON is the founder and principle consultant of Build You Up!, LLC (BYU). The firm's mission of "growing to higher heights within" is the driving force behind her life's work. Jamie specializes in personal core development—applying therapeutic techniques to business. Her clientele roster includes athletes, business leaders, owners, and aspiring entrepreneurs. Jamie heads BYU initiatives: Build You Up Sisters, an online platform for mothers across the globe where trust, encouragement, relationships and support form a sisterhood; and Build You Up Academy, an online training and education center where students are trained in group leadership, business basics, and personal development.

Jamie has twenty years of experience working with non-profit organizations. Her love for edifying people has been evident through her work with at-risk youth, preventing families from becoming involved in the child welfare system, and through establishing partnerships to revitalize communities through entrepreneurship. She also serves as the Board Chair for G.O girls, Inc. a non-profit organization that assists and provides resources and support for young women transitioning out of foster care.

A Pittsburgh native, Jamie holds a Bachelor of Arts degree in Psychology with a minor in Sociology from Edinboro University of Pennsylvania. She went on to attend Duquesne University and obtain a Master of Science Education, majoring in Marriage and Family Therapy. Jamie's greatest accomplishment to date is the honor of raising an energetic, always happy boy, Caleb, alongside her love, Joshua. She is the author of *Strong Faith: Daily Encouragement for Moms and Families of Premature Babies*, which was inspired by her resilient son, Caleb.

To learn more about Jamie and Build You Up Sisters, visit *byusisters.buildyouup.org* and connect with the Sisterhood on social media @byusisters.

Made in the USA
Columbia, SC
19 September 2022